Finding a Balance

A Weekly Planner for Your Inner Yogi

Activinotes

Activinotes

DAILY JOURNALS, PLANNERS, NOTEBOOKS AND OTHER BLANK BOOKS

Weekly Planner

MONDAY	TUESDAY	WEDNESDAY
THURSDAY	FRIDAY	SATURDAY

SUNDAY

Meditation

Notes :

Weekly Planner

☯ Weekly Planner ☾

MONDAY	TUESDAY	WEDNESDAY
THURSDAY	FRIDAY	SATURDAY

SUNDAY

Meditation

Notes :

Weekly Planner

Weekly Planner

MONDAY	TUESDAY	WEDNESDAY
THURSDAY	FRIDAY	SATURDAY

SUNDAY

Meditation

Notes :

Weekly Planner

☯ Weekly Planner ☯

MONDAY	TUESDAY	WEDNESDAY
THURSDAY	FRIDAY	SATURDAY

SUNDAY

Meditation

Notes :

Weekly Planner

Weekly Planner

MONDAY	TUESDAY	WEDNESDAY

THURSDAY	FRIDAY	SATURDAY

SUNDAY

Meditation

Notes :

Weekly Planner

☯ Weekly Planner ☯

MONDAY	TUESDAY	WEDNESDAY
THURSDAY	FRIDAY	SATURDAY

SUNDAY

Meditation

Notes :

Weekly Planner

Weekly Planner

MONDAY	TUESDAY	WEDNESDAY
THURSDAY	FRIDAY	SATURDAY

SUNDAY

Meditation

Notes :

Weekly Planner

☯ Weekly Planner ☯

MONDAY	TUESDAY	WEDNESDAY
THURSDAY	FRIDAY	SATURDAY

SUNDAY

Meditation

Notes :

Weekly Planner

☯ Weekly Planner ☯

MONDAY	TUESDAY	WEDNESDAY
THURSDAY	FRIDAY	SATURDAY

SUNDAY

Notes :

Meditation

Weekly Planner

Weekly Planner

MONDAY	TUESDAY	WEDNESDAY

THURSDAY	FRIDAY	SATURDAY

SUNDAY

Meditation

Notes :

Weekly Planner

Weekly Planner

MONDAY	TUESDAY	WEDNESDAY
THURSDAY	FRIDAY	SATURDAY

SUNDAY

Meditation

Notes :

Weekly Planner

☯ Weekly Planner ☯

MONDAY	TUESDAY	WEDNESDAY
THURSDAY	FRIDAY	SATURDAY

SUNDAY

Meditation

Notes :

Weekly Planner

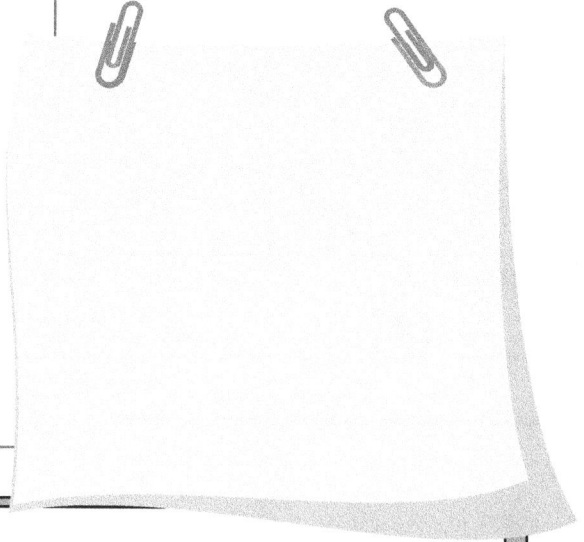

Weekly Planner

MONDAY	TUESDAY	WEDNESDAY
THURSDAY	FRIDAY	SATURDAY

SUNDAY

Meditation

Notes:

Weekly Planner

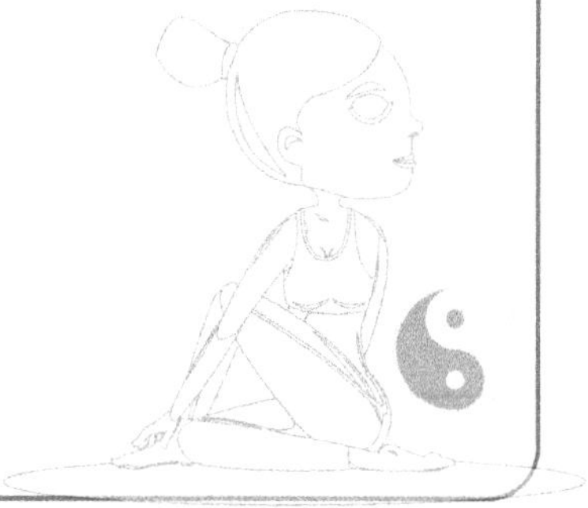

☯ Weekly Planner ☯

MONDAY	TUESDAY	WEDNESDAY
THURSDAY	FRIDAY	SATURDAY

SUNDAY

Notes :

Meditation

Weekly Planner

Weekly Planner

MONDAY	TUESDAY	WEDNESDAY

THURSDAY	FRIDAY	SATURDAY

SUNDAY

Notes :

Meditation

Weekly Planner

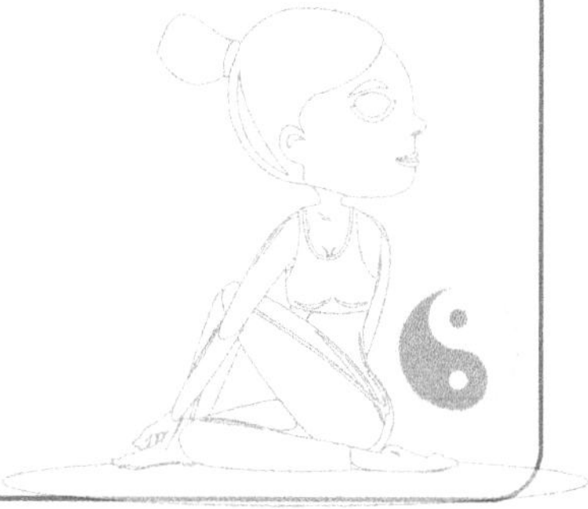

☯ Weekly Planner ☯

MONDAY	TUESDAY	WEDNESDAY
THURSDAY	FRIDAY	SATURDAY

SUNDAY

Meditation

Notes :

Weekly Planner

Weekly Planner

MONDAY	TUESDAY	WEDNESDAY
THURSDAY	FRIDAY	SATURDAY

SUNDAY

Notes :

Meditation

Weekly Planner

Weekly Planner

MONDAY	TUESDAY	WEDNESDAY
THURSDAY	FRIDAY	SATURDAY

SUNDAY

Notes :

Meditation

Weekly Planner

Weekly Planner

MONDAY	TUESDAY	WEDNESDAY

THURSDAY	FRIDAY	SATURDAY

SUNDAY

Meditation

Notes :

Weekly Planner

Weekly Planner

MONDAY	TUESDAY	WEDNESDAY
THURSDAY	FRIDAY	SATURDAY

SUNDAY

Notes :

Meditation

Weekly Planner

Weekly Planner

MONDAY	TUESDAY	WEDNESDAY
THURSDAY	FRIDAY	SATURDAY

SUNDAY

Meditation

Notes :

Weekly Planner

Weekly Planner

MONDAY	TUESDAY	WEDNESDAY

THURSDAY	FRIDAY	SATURDAY

SUNDAY

Notes:

Meditation

Weekly Planner

Weekly Planner

MONDAY	TUESDAY	WEDNESDAY

THURSDAY	FRIDAY	SATURDAY

SUNDAY

Meditation

Notes :

Weekly Planner

Weekly Planner

MONDAY	TUESDAY	WEDNESDAY

THURSDAY	FRIDAY	SATURDAY

SUNDAY

Notes:

Meditation

Weekly Planner

Weekly Planner

MONDAY	TUESDAY	WEDNESDAY

THURSDAY	FRIDAY	SATURDAY

SUNDAY

Meditation

Notes:

Weekly Planner

Weekly Planner

MONDAY	TUESDAY	WEDNESDAY
THURSDAY	FRIDAY	SATURDAY

SUNDAY

Meditation

Notes :

Weekly Planner

Weekly Planner

MONDAY	TUESDAY	WEDNESDAY
THURSDAY	FRIDAY	SATURDAY

SUNDAY

Meditation

Notes :

Weekly Planner

☯ Weekly Planner ☯

MONDAY	TUESDAY	WEDNESDAY
THURSDAY	FRIDAY	SATURDAY

SUNDAY

Meditation

Notes :

Weekly Planner

Weekly Planner

MONDAY	TUESDAY	WEDNESDAY
THURSDAY	FRIDAY	SATURDAY

SUNDAY

Meditation

Notes :

Weekly Planner

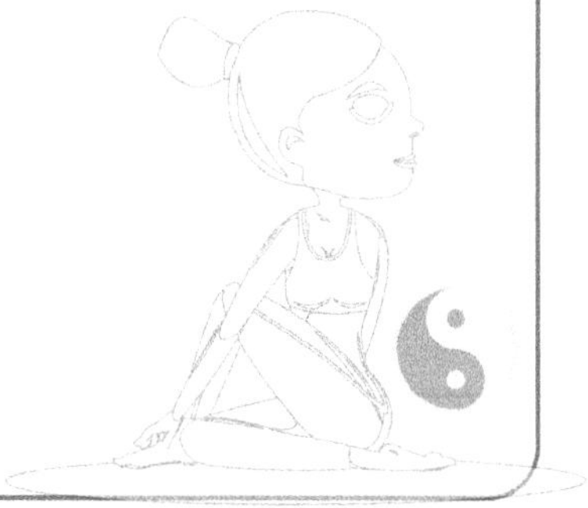

Weekly Planner

MONDAY	TUESDAY	WEDNESDAY
THURSDAY	FRIDAY	SATURDAY

SUNDAY

Meditation

Notes :

Weekly Planner

☯ Weekly Planner ☯

MONDAY	TUESDAY	WEDNESDAY
THURSDAY	FRIDAY	SATURDAY

SUNDAY

Meditation

Notes:

Weekly Planner

☯ Weekly Planner ☯

MONDAY	TUESDAY	WEDNESDAY
THURSDAY	FRIDAY	SATURDAY

SUNDAY

Notes :

Meditation

Weekly Planner

Weekly Planner

MONDAY	TUESDAY	WEDNESDAY

THURSDAY	FRIDAY	SATURDAY

SUNDAY

Meditation

Notes:

Weekly Planner

☯ Weekly Planner ☯

MONDAY	TUESDAY	WEDNESDAY
THURSDAY	FRIDAY	SATURDAY

SUNDAY

Meditation

Notes :

Weekly Planner

☯ Weekly Planner ☯

MONDAY	TUESDAY	WEDNESDAY

THURSDAY	FRIDAY	SATURDAY

SUNDAY

Meditation

Notes :

Weekly Planner

Weekly Planner

MONDAY	TUESDAY	WEDNESDAY

THURSDAY	FRIDAY	SATURDAY

SUNDAY

Meditation

Notes :

Weekly Planner

Weekly Planner

MONDAY	TUESDAY	WEDNESDAY
THURSDAY	FRIDAY	SATURDAY

SUNDAY

Meditation

Notes :

Weekly Planner

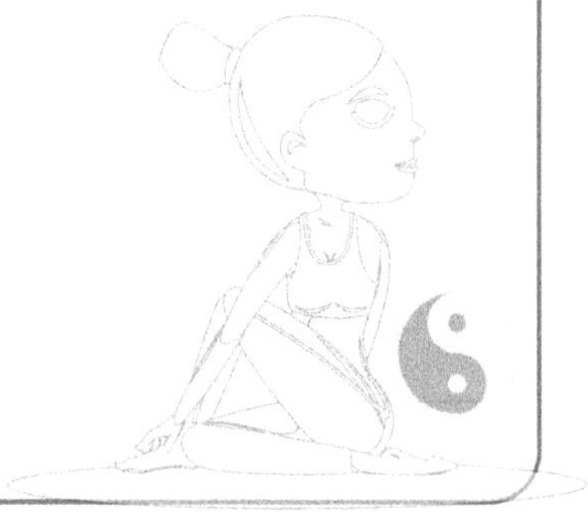

Weekly Planner

MONDAY	TUESDAY	WEDNESDAY
THURSDAY	FRIDAY	SATURDAY

SUNDAY

Meditation

Notes :

Weekly Planner

Weekly Planner

MONDAY	TUESDAY	WEDNESDAY
THURSDAY	FRIDAY	SATURDAY

SUNDAY

Meditation

Notes :

Weekly Planner

Weekly Planner

MONDAY	TUESDAY	WEDNESDAY
THURSDAY	FRIDAY	SATURDAY

SUNDAY

Notes:

Meditation

Weekly Planner

Weekly Planner

MONDAY	TUESDAY	WEDNESDAY

THURSDAY	FRIDAY	SATURDAY

SUNDAY

Meditation

Notes :

Weekly Planner

☯ Weekly Planner ☯

MONDAY	TUESDAY	WEDNESDAY
THURSDAY	FRIDAY	SATURDAY

SUNDAY

Meditation

Notes :

Weekly Planner

Weekly Planner

MONDAY	TUESDAY	WEDNESDAY

THURSDAY	FRIDAY	SATURDAY

SUNDAY

Notes:

Meditation

Weekly Planner

Weekly Planner

MONDAY	TUESDAY	WEDNESDAY

THURSDAY | FRIDAY | SATURDAY

SUNDAY

Meditation

Notes :

Weekly Planner

Weekly Planner

MONDAY	TUESDAY	WEDNESDAY
THURSDAY	FRIDAY	SATURDAY

SUNDAY

Meditation

Notes:

Weekly Planner

Weekly Planner

MONDAY	TUESDAY	WEDNESDAY

THURSDAY	FRIDAY	SATURDAY

SUNDAY

Meditation

Notes :

Weekly Planner

Weekly Planner

MONDAY	TUESDAY	WEDNESDAY

THURSDAY	FRIDAY	SATURDAY

SUNDAY

Meditation

Notes:

Weekly Planner

☯ Weekly Planner ☯

MONDAY	TUESDAY	WEDNESDAY

THURSDAY	FRIDAY	SATURDAY

SUNDAY

Notes :

Meditation

Weekly Planner

☯ Weekly Planner ☯

MONDAY	TUESDAY	WEDNESDAY
THURSDAY	FRIDAY	SATURDAY

SUNDAY

Meditation

Notes:

Weekly Planner

Weekly Planner

MONDAY	TUESDAY	WEDNESDAY

THURSDAY	FRIDAY	SATURDAY

SUNDAY

Notes :

Meditation

Weekly Planner

Weekly Planner

MONDAY	TUESDAY	WEDNESDAY
THURSDAY	FRIDAY	SATURDAY

SUNDAY

Meditation

Notes:

Weekly Planner

Weekly Planner

MONDAY	TUESDAY	WEDNESDAY

THURSDAY	FRIDAY	SATURDAY

SUNDAY

Meditation

Notes :

Weekly Planner

Weekly Planner

MONDAY	TUESDAY	WEDNESDAY

THURSDAY	FRIDAY	SATURDAY

SUNDAY

Meditation

Notes :

Weekly Planner

Weekly Planner

MONDAY	TUESDAY	WEDNESDAY
THURSDAY	FRIDAY	SATURDAY

SUNDAY

Meditation

Notes :

Weekly Planner

Weekly Planner

MONDAY	TUESDAY	WEDNESDAY

THURSDAY	FRIDAY	SATURDAY

SUNDAY

Meditation

Notes:

Weekly Planner

☯ Weekly Planner ☯

MONDAY	TUESDAY	WEDNESDAY
THURSDAY	FRIDAY	SATURDAY

SUNDAY

Meditation

Notes :

Weekly Planner

Notes

www.ingramcontent.com/pod-product-compliance
Lightning Source LLC
Chambersburg PA
CBHW080519090426
42734CB00015B/3112